Dream by Dream

The Story of Rabbi Isaac Mayer Wise

For Andrea Rapp, who knew from the start that Isaac Mayer Wise's life story belonged in the hands of young readers, and for her faith in my ability to help make it happen. And in loving memory of my mother, who lived her dream. —G.K.

To my family —S.M.

Acknowledgements
Wiith grateful appreciation to Rabbi Lewis H. Kamrass for lending his expertise, and to the Jacob Raider Marcus Center of the American Jewish Archives at Hebrew Union College-Jewish Institute of Religion—specifically to Dr. Gary P. Zola for his belief in this project, for generously sharing his wealth of knowledge, and for his patient and instant responses to my many questions. Thanks also to the Roots of Reform Judaism for its vote of confidence, specifically to Rabbi Ken Kanter for his enthusiastic cheerleading. With deep gratitude to Joni Sussman and the Kar-Ben team for taking a chance on me and on this story. Finally, with heartfelt thanks to Isaac Mayer Wise, of blessed memory, whose colorful life and countless accomplishments inspired this story. I hope we have done justice to his legacy. —G.K.

KAR-BEN PUBLISHING®
An imprint of Lerner Publishing Group, Inc.
241 First Avenue North
Minneapolis, MN 55401 USA
Website address: www.karben.com

Image credits: National Portrait Gallery, Smithsonian Institution; gift of the Hebrew Union College (CC0 1.0), p. 30 (top); Pictures Now/Alamy Stock Photo, p. 30 (bottom).

Main body text set in Oldbook ITC Std
Typeface provided by International Typeface Corp

Library of Congress Cataloging-in-Publication Data

Names: Kolesar, Geri, author. | Moore, Sofia, 1969- illustrator.
Title: Dream by dream : the story of Rabbi Isaac Mayer Wise / Geri Kolesar ; illustrated by Sofia Moore.
Description: Minneapolis, MN : Kar-Ben Publishing ®, [2023] | Audience: Ages 5–10 | Audience: Grades 2–3 | Summary: Story of Rabbi Isaac Mayer Wise, founder of American Reform Judaism.
Identifiers: LCCN 2022040487 (print) | LCCN 2022040488 (ebook) | ISBN 9781728467931 (library binding) | ISBN 9781728467948 (paperback) | ISBN 9781728495507 (ebook)
Subjects: LCSH: Wise, Isaac Mayer, 1819-1900—Juvenile literature. | Rabbis—United States—Biography—Juvenile literature. | Reform Judaism—United States—History—19th century—Juvenile literature.
Classification: LCC BM755.W5 K65 2023 (print) | LCC BM755.W5 (ebook) | DDC 296.092 [B]—dc23/eng/20220822

LC record available at https://lccn.loc.gov/2022040487
LC ebook record available at https://lccn.loc.gov/2022040488

Manufactured in the United States of America
1-51835-50462-11/29/2022

Dream by Dream

The Story of Rabbi Isaac Mayer Wise

Geri Kolesar

illustrated by Sofia Moore

KAR-BEN
PUBLISHING

In 1819, in a small Bohemian village, a poor Jewish schoolteacher and his wife welcomed a son into the world. They blessed him and named him Isaac.

Life was not easy for Jews in this part of Europe. They couldn't own land or live in certain places. They often faced hatred and harsh treatment. Isaac's parents dreamed of a world where their son would have the same freedoms as his neighbors.

Isaac's father was a teacher, and Isaac was a curious child, eager to learn. Instead of playing with the neighborhood children, he followed his father to the tiny schoolroom in their house. Before long, Isaac could read as well as the older students. To Isaac, written words were magic keys unlocking new worlds.

One day, the butcher's son hit Isaac, just because Isaac was Jewish. Isaac hit back. Isaac expected his father to praise his courage, but his father scolded him.

Instead of using fists, he would need to use words, said his father. So Isaac filled his head with more and more words.

It wasn't long before his
father's school was too easy for
Isaac, but his parents had no money for
private tutors. So with heavy hearts, they sent
six-year-old Isaac to live with his grandfather, a
doctor, in a village with a more challenging school.

Isaac missed his parents, but he grew to love and admire his grandfather. During the day, Isaac attended school while his grandfather treated patients. At night, his grandfather took out books and taught Isaac about the works of leading Jewish thinkers.

Isaac wanted to keep learning and to help others learn.
His grandfather told him about a city called Prague
where Jews from all over the world gathered to study.
Isaac dreamed of going there and becoming a rabbi.

When Isaac was twelve, his grandfather died. Isaac decided he would honor his grandfather's memory by following his dreams. He walked all the way to Prague with only a small bundle of clothes and a few coins.

In Prague, Isaac lived with Jewish families who took in
students. He spent each day of the week in a different family's
home. He studied hard at the Jewish school. It was a small,
simple building. But to Isaac, it was a castle of promise.

Soon, the whole Jewish community knew about the eager, talented young student. When he was sixteen, he began training as a rabbi. He loved learning. He went to the university, taught himself other languages, studied other religions, and learned to play the violin. He studied literature and science.

Isaac began building a life for himself. He became a rabbi. He married a bright young woman named Therese. And he got a job at a synagogue in a small town.

The congregation expected an old-fashioned rabbi. But Isaac did things differently. When he gave sermons, instead of writing down what he planned to say ahead of time, he spoke from the heart. And he questioned some of the old customs.

Isaac believed that girls should have the opportunity to learn about their Jewish heritage, just as boys did. He also thought that women should be treated as equal members of the congregation and that families should be able to worship together.

His congregants didn't agree. They refused to change their traditions.

Meanwhile, Isaac was hearing more and more about America, a place that welcomed new ideas. Perhaps Isaac's dreams for Judaism would fit better in this faraway land.

In 1846, Isaac, Therese, and their baby daughter boarded a ship heading to New York City. They sailed for two months, through good weather and bad, across the Atlantic Ocean.

When Isaac's family arrived in America, there were only a few trained rabbis in the whole country. One of them, Rabbi Max Lilienthal, became Isaac's friend. He encouraged Isaac to travel around and lead services for different congregations looking for rabbis.

Isaac impressed those congregations. He was invited to become the rabbi for a congregation in Albany, New York.

Isaac noticed that Jews in Albany didn't mingle with their non-Jewish neighbors.

He thought people should get to know their neighbors, learn about different cultures and religions in their city, and pay attention to what was happening outside the Jewish community.

Isaac started giving his sermons in English instead of German.

Boys and girls were welcome to study together and to sing together in the choir.

Many people supported these changes, but others didn't like the young rabbi's changes. Isaac soon realized he was dividing the community he had hoped to unite.

Leaders of a congregation in Cincinnati, Ohio, heard about Isaac and his new ideas. They invited Isaac to become their rabbi.

Isaac got to work at his new synagogue. He brought new music to the service and conducted a choir of men and women. He even played his violin when conducting the choir in the synagogue.

He also tried to be a good neighbor. He and Therese opened their home to people going through hard times, sharing their food and money with those in need, as others had once done for him.

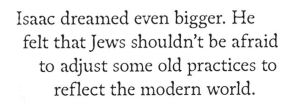

Isaac dreamed even bigger. He felt that Jews shouldn't be afraid to adjust some old practices to reflect the modern world.

He thought every religion had truth in it, and that Jews could respect their neighbors of different faiths. And he believed science could exist alongside religion without threatening it.

He started a Jewish newspaper so he could share his creative ideas with Jews throughout America. He published novels, plays, and short stories featuring Jewish characters and modern themes. Many Jews were excited to be part of the changes Isaac was writing about.

Isaac's congregation grew. It was time to build a bigger synagogue. Isaac wanted the new synagogue to be equal to any other place of worship in America. Plum Street Temple was built on a busy corner, across from Cincinnati's City Hall and near two Christian churches.

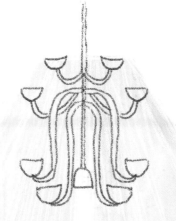

Isaac organized meetings of Jewish leaders from around the country.
He encouraged people to share ideas, even if they ended up disagreeing.
He dreamed of starting a college to train new rabbis.

When Isaac made this dream a reality, his old friend Max was by his side, teaching Hebrew Union College's first classes. Isaac paid the tuition for some of the poorest students. Isaac opened the school's doors to young women. He believed women should have a chance to become rabbis, though it wasn't until many years later that the college began ordaining women.

Isaac wasn't afraid of change. He fought for his beliefs.
And he never forgot the many generous people who helped him.

His ideas live on, inspiring
others to pursue their dreams.

Author's Note

Rabbi Isaac Mayer Wise

From the time he was a young boy in Bohemia—present day Czech Republic—through his old age in the United States, Isaac Mayer Wise fought for fairness and religious freedom. He dreamed of modernizing Judaism but realized Jews did not all want to be unified under a single tent. Instead, he played a central role in creating a new branch of Judaism, American Reform Judaism.

In 1846, when Isaac arrived in America, there were no national Jewish organizations. Isaac helped build institutions that continue to support Reform Judaism today. He established *The American Israelite*, a weekly Jewish newspaper still in print. He started the Central Conference of American Rabbis and the Union of American Hebrew Congregations, now known as the Union for Reform Judaism. And he founded Hebrew Union College (HUC), the first institution of higher Jewish learning in America, and served as its first president until his death. Continuing Isaac's fight for fairness, HUC ordained the United States' first woman rabbi, Sally Priesand, in 1972. Today, the school Isaac started is open to people of all faiths and promotes understanding between people of all ethnic and religious backgrounds.

His fight for religious freedom was the thread stringing together Isaac's dreams. When Plum Street Temple was built, Isaac made sure to place a Bible wrapped in an American flag under the first cornerstone as a symbol of this country's religious freedom.

I treasure what Judaism has brought to my life. I am especially thankful for the Cincinnati congregation Isaac Mayer Wise built, which has welcomed my interfaith family with open arms. I am honored to share his story with you.

The Plum Street Temple, Cincinnati, Ohio

TIMELINE OF ISAAC'S LIFE & LEGACY

1819   Isaac is born on March 29.

1842   Isaac is ordained as a rabbi.

1844   Isaac marries Therese Bloch.

1846   Isaac arrives in New York and becomes the rabbi for Congregation Beth El in Albany.

1854   Isaac arrives in Cincinnati, Ohio, to become rabbi of K.K. B'nai Yeshurun.

1854   Isaac publishes *The Israelite* (later renamed *The American Israelite*), an English-language Jewish newspaper.

1866   Construction of Plum Street Temple is completed.

1873   Isaac founds the Union of American Hebrew Congregations (now the Union for Reform Judaism).

1874   Therese Bloch dies.

1875   Hebrew Union College opens. Isaac is elected president.

1876   Isaac marries Selma Bondi.

1889   Isaac founds and is elected president of Central Conference of American Rabbis (CCAR).

1900   Isaac dies on March 26. His pulpit chair at Plum Street Temple is draped in black and kept vacant for a year.

1931   K.K. B'nai Yeshurun becomes known as Isaac M. Wise Temple.

1975   Plum Street Temple is designated a National Historic Landmark.

2019   Isaac is inducted into the Jewish-American Hall of Fame, joining icons such as Albert Einstein, Barbra Streisand, and Ruth Bader Ginsburg.

About the Author

In addition to writing for children, **Geri Kolesar** has taught environmental education, worked for a United States Senator on Capitol Hill, and practiced law. She lives in Cincinnati, Ohio.

About the Illustrator

Sofia Moore is a Ukrainian-American artist and illustrator based in Las Vegas, Nevada. She grew up reading folktales in her grandmother's house and drawing princesses on the back of textbooks. She loves painting traditionally, but also layers textures both on paper and digitally.